This mileage tracker belongs to:

Mileage TRACKER

PERIOD OF:

DATE:	TO:	FROM:	PURPOSE:	TOTAL DISTANCE

Mileage TRACKER

PERIOD OF:

DATE:	TO:	FROM:	PURPOSE:	TOTAL DISTANCE

Mileage TRACKER

PERIOD OF:

DATE:	TO:	FROM:	PURPOSE:	TOTAL DISTANCE

Mileage TRACKER

PERIOD OF:

DATE:	TO:	FROM:	PURPOSE:	TOTAL DISTANCE

Mileage TRACKER

PERIOD OF:

DATE:	TO:	FROM:	PURPOSE:	TOTAL DISTANCE

Mileage TRACKER

PERIOD OF:

DATE:	TO:	FROM:	PURPOSE:	TOTAL DISTANCE

Mileage TRACKER

PERIOD OF:

DATE:	TO:	FROM:	PURPOSE:	TOTAL DISTANCE

Mileage TRACKER

PERIOD OF:

DATE:	TO:	FROM:	PURPOSE:	TOTAL DISTANCE

Mileage TRACKER

DATE:	TO:	FROM:	PURPOSE:	TOTAL DISTANCE

Mileage TRACKER

PERIOD OF:

DATE:	TO:	FROM:	PURPOSE:	TOTAL DISTANCE

Mileage TRACKER

PERIOD OF:

DATE:	TO:	FROM:	PURPOSE:	TOTAL DISTANCE

Mileage TRACKER

PERIOD OF:

DATE:	TO:	FROM:	PURPOSE:	TOTAL DISTANCE

Mileage TRACKER

PERIOD OF:

DATE: **TO:**   **FROM:**   **PURPOSE:**   **TOTAL DISTANCE**

Mileage TRACKER

PERIOD OF:

DATE:	TO:	FROM:	PURPOSE:	TOTAL DISTANCE

Mileage TRACKER

PERIOD OF:

DATE:	TO:	FROM:	PURPOSE:	TOTAL DISTANCE

Mileage TRACKER

PERIOD OF:

DATE:	TO:	FROM:	PURPOSE:	TOTAL DISTANCE

Mileage TRACKER

PERIOD OF:

DATE:	TO:	FROM:	PURPOSE:	TOTAL DISTANCE

Mileage TRACKER

PERIOD OF:

DATE:	TO:	FROM:	PURPOSE:	TOTAL DISTANCE

Mileage TRACKER

PERIOD OF:

DATE:	TO:	FROM:	PURPOSE:	TOTAL DISTANCE

Mileage TRACKER

PERIOD OF:

DATE:	TO:	FROM:	PURPOSE:	TOTAL DISTANCE

Mileage TRACKER

PERIOD OF:

DATE: TO: FROM: PURPOSE: TOTAL DISTANCE

Mileage TRACKER

PERIOD OF:

DATE:	TO:	FROM:	PURPOSE:	TOTAL DISTANCE

Mileage TRACKER

PERIOD OF:

DATE: **TO:**   **FROM:**   **PURPOSE:**   **TOTAL DISTANCE**

Mileage TRACKER

PERIOD OF:

DATE:	TO:	FROM:	PURPOSE:	TOTAL DISTANCE

Mileage TRACKER

PERIOD OF:

DATE:	TO:	FROM:	PURPOSE:	TOTAL DISTANCE

Mileage TRACKER

PERIOD OF:

DATE:	TO:	FROM:	PURPOSE:	TOTAL DISTANCE

Mileage TRACKER

PERIOD OF:

DATE:	TO:	FROM:	PURPOSE:	TOTAL DISTANCE

Mileage TRACKER

PERIOD OF:

DATE:	TO:	FROM:	PURPOSE:	TOTAL DISTANCE

Mileage TRACKER

PERIOD OF:

DATE:	TO:	FROM:	PURPOSE:	TOTAL DISTANCE

Mileage TRACKER

PERIOD OF:

DATE:	TO:	FROM:	PURPOSE:	TOTAL DISTANCE

Mileage TRACKER

PERIOD OF:

DATE:	TO:	FROM:	PURPOSE:	TOTAL DISTANCE

Mileage TRACKER

PERIOD OF:

DATE:	TO:	FROM:	PURPOSE:	TOTAL DISTANCE

Mileage TRACKER

PERIOD OF:

DATE:	TO:	FROM:	PURPOSE:	TOTAL DISTANCE

Mileage TRACKER

PERIOD OF:

DATE:	TO:	FROM:	PURPOSE:	TOTAL DISTANCE

Mileage TRACKER

PERIOD OF:

DATE: **TO:**   **FROM:**   **PURPOSE:**   **TOTAL DISTANCE**

Mileage TRACKER

PERIOD OF:

DATE:	TO:	FROM:	PURPOSE:	TOTAL DISTANCE

Mileage TRACKER

PERIOD OF:

DATE:	TO:	FROM:	PURPOSE:	TOTAL DISTANCE

Mileage TRACKER

PERIOD OF:

DATE:	TO:	FROM:	PURPOSE:	TOTAL DISTANCE

Mileage TRACKER

PERIOD OF:

DATE: **TO:**   **FROM:**   **PURPOSE:**   **TOTAL DISTANCE**

Mileage TRACKER

PERIOD OF:

DATE:	TO:	FROM:	PURPOSE:	TOTAL DISTANCE

Mileage TRACKER

PERIOD OF:

DATE:	TO:	FROM:	PURPOSE:	TOTAL DISTANCE

Mileage TRACKER

PERIOD OF:

DATE:	TO:	FROM:	PURPOSE:	TOTAL DISTANCE

Mileage TRACKER

PERIOD OF:

DATE:	TO:	FROM:	PURPOSE:	TOTAL DISTANCE

Mileage TRACKER

PERIOD OF:

DATE:	TO:	FROM:	PURPOSE:	TOTAL DISTANCE

Mileage TRACKER

PERIOD OF:

DATE:	TO:	FROM:	PURPOSE:	TOTAL DISTANCE

Mileage TRACKER

PERIOD OF:

DATE:	TO:	FROM:	PURPOSE:	TOTAL DISTANCE

Mileage TRACKER

PERIOD OF:

DATE:	TO:	FROM:	PURPOSE:	TOTAL DISTANCE

Mileage TRACKER

PERIOD OF:

DATE:	TO:	FROM:	PURPOSE:	TOTAL DISTANCE

Mileage TRACKER

PERIOD OF:

DATE:	TO:	FROM:	PURPOSE:	TOTAL DISTANCE

Mileage TRACKER

PERIOD OF:

DATE:	TO:	FROM:	PURPOSE:	TOTAL DISTANCE

Mileage TRACKER

PERIOD OF:

DATE:	TO:	FROM:	PURPOSE:	TOTAL DISTANCE

Mileage TRACKER

PERIOD OF:

DATE:	TO:	FROM:	PURPOSE:	TOTAL DISTANCE

Mileage TRACKER

PERIOD OF:

DATE:	TO:	FROM:	PURPOSE:	TOTAL DISTANCE

Mileage TRACKER

PERIOD OF:

DATE:	TO:	FROM:	PURPOSE:	TOTAL DISTANCE

Mileage TRACKER

PERIOD OF:

DATE: **TO:**   **FROM:**   **PURPOSE:**   **TOTAL DISTANCE**

Mileage TRACKER

PERIOD OF:

DATE:	TO:	FROM:	PURPOSE:	TOTAL DISTANCE

Mileage TRACKER

DATE:	TO:	FROM:	PURPOSE:	TOTAL DISTANCE

Mileage TRACKER

PERIOD OF:

DATE:	TO:	FROM:	PURPOSE:	TOTAL DISTANCE

Mileage TRACKER

PERIOD OF:

DATE:	TO:	FROM:	PURPOSE:	TOTAL DISTANCE

Mileage TRACKER

PERIOD OF:

DATE:	TO:	FROM:	PURPOSE:	TOTAL DISTANCE

Mileage TRACKER

PERIOD OF:

DATE:	TO:	FROM:	PURPOSE:	TOTAL DISTANCE

Mileage TRACKER

PERIOD OF:

DATE:	TO:	FROM:	PURPOSE:	TOTAL DISTANCE

Mileage TRACKER

PERIOD OF:

DATE:	TO:	FROM:	PURPOSE:	TOTAL DISTANCE

Mileage TRACKER

PERIOD OF:

DATE:	TO:	FROM:	PURPOSE:	TOTAL DISTANCE

Mileage TRACKER

PERIOD OF:

DATE:	TO:	FROM:	PURPOSE:	TOTAL DISTANCE

Mileage TRACKER

PERIOD OF:

DATE:	TO:	FROM:	PURPOSE:	TOTAL DISTANCE

Mileage TRACKER

PERIOD OF:

DATE:	TO:	FROM:	PURPOSE:	TOTAL DISTANCE

Mileage TRACKER

PERIOD OF:

DATE:	TO:	FROM:	PURPOSE:	TOTAL DISTANCE

Mileage TRACKER

PERIOD OF:

DATE:	TO:	FROM:	PURPOSE:	TOTAL DISTANCE

Mileage TRACKER

PERIOD OF:

DATE:	TO:	FROM:	PURPOSE:	TOTAL DISTANCE

Mileage TRACKER

PERIOD OF:

DATE:	TO:	FROM:	PURPOSE:	TOTAL DISTANCE

Mileage TRACKER

PERIOD OF:

DATE:	TO:	FROM:	PURPOSE:	TOTAL DISTANCE

Mileage TRACKER

PERIOD OF:

DATE:	TO:	FROM:	PURPOSE:	TOTAL DISTANCE

Mileage TRACKER

PERIOD OF:

DATE:	TO:	FROM:	PURPOSE:	TOTAL DISTANCE

Mileage TRACKER

PERIOD OF:

DATE:	TO:	FROM:	PURPOSE:	TOTAL DISTANCE

Mileage TRACKER

PERIOD OF:

DATE:	TO:	FROM:	PURPOSE:	TOTAL DISTANCE

Mileage TRACKER

PERIOD OF:

DATE:	TO:	FROM:	PURPOSE:	TOTAL DISTANCE

Mileage TRACKER

PERIOD OF:

DATE:	TO:	FROM:	PURPOSE:	TOTAL DISTANCE

Mileage TRACKER

PERIOD OF:

DATE:	TO:	FROM:	PURPOSE:	TOTAL DISTANCE

Mileage TRACKER

PERIOD OF:

DATE:	TO:	FROM:	PURPOSE:	TOTAL DISTANCE

Mileage TRACKER

PERIOD OF:

DATE:	TO:	FROM:	PURPOSE:	TOTAL DISTANCE

Mileage TRACKER

PERIOD OF:

DATE:	TO:	FROM:	PURPOSE:	TOTAL DISTANCE

Mileage TRACKER

PERIOD OF:

DATE:	TO:	FROM:	PURPOSE:	TOTAL DISTANCE

Mileage TRACKER

PERIOD OF:

DATE:	TO:	FROM:	PURPOSE:	TOTAL DISTANCE

Mileage TRACKER

PERIOD OF:

DATE:	TO:	FROM:	PURPOSE:	TOTAL DISTANCE

Mileage TRACKER

PERIOD OF:

DATE:	TO:	FROM:	PURPOSE:	TOTAL DISTANCE

Mileage TRACKER

PERIOD OF:

DATE: **TO:**   **FROM:**   **PURPOSE:**   **TOTAL DISTANCE**

Mileage TRACKER

PERIOD OF:

DATE: **TO:**   **FROM:**   **PURPOSE:**   **TOTAL DISTANCE**

Mileage TRACKER

PERIOD OF:

DATE:	TO:	FROM:	PURPOSE:	TOTAL DISTANCE

Mileage TRACKER

PERIOD OF:

DATE: **TO:**   **FROM:**   **PURPOSE:**   **TOTAL DISTANCE**

Mileage TRACKER

PERIOD OF:

DATE:	TO:	FROM:	PURPOSE:	TOTAL DISTANCE

Mileage TRACKER

PERIOD OF:

DATE:	TO:	FROM:	PURPOSE:	TOTAL DISTANCE

Mileage TRACKER

PERIOD OF:

DATE:	TO:	FROM:	PURPOSE:	TOTAL DISTANCE

Mileage TRACKER

PERIOD OF:

DATE:	TO:	FROM:	PURPOSE:	TOTAL DISTANCE

Mileage TRACKER

PERIOD OF:

DATE:	TO:	FROM:	PURPOSE:	TOTAL DISTANCE

Mileage TRACKER

PERIOD OF:

DATE:	TO:	FROM:	PURPOSE:	TOTAL DISTANCE

Mileage TRACKER

PERIOD OF:

DATE:	TO:	FROM:	PURPOSE:	TOTAL DISTANCE

Mileage TRACKER

PERIOD OF:

DATE:	TO:	FROM:	PURPOSE:	TOTAL DISTANCE

Mileage TRACKER

PERIOD OF:

DATE:	TO:	FROM:	PURPOSE:	TOTAL DISTANCE

Mileage TRACKER

PERIOD OF:

DATE:	TO:	FROM:	PURPOSE:	TOTAL DISTANCE

www.ingramcontent.com/pod-product-compliance
Lightning Source LLC
Chambersburg PA
CBHW081523220526
45467CB00010B/3024